Robinson Crusoe's Diary

Abridged by Sue Hackman

HODDER EDUCATION
PART OF HACHETTE LIVRE UK

The Publishers would like to thank the following for permission to reproduce copyright material:
Photo credits
p.ii © Hulton Archive/Getty Images; **p.v** © Mary Evans Picture Library/Alamy; **p.vii** © Mary Evans Picture Library; **p.2** © akg-images; **p.6** © Archivo Iconografico, SA/Corbis; **p.9** © Private Collection/The Bridgeman Art Library; **p.13** © Lebrecht Music and Arts Photo Library/Alamy; **p.18** © Steve Wilkings/Corbis; **p.23** © Bettmann/Corbis; **pp.17, 27** © TopFoto/HIP

Every effort has been made to trace all copyright holders, but if any have been inadvertently overlooked the Publishers will be pleased to make the necessary arrangements at the first opportunity.

Hachette Livre UK's policy is to use papers that are natural, renewable and recyclable products and made from wood grown in sustainable forests. The logging and manufacturing processes are expected to conform to the environmental regulations of the country of origin.

Orders: please contact Bookpoint Ltd, 130 Milton Park, Abingdon, Oxon OX14 4SB. Telephone: (44) 01235 827720. Fax: (44) 01235 400454. Lines are open from 9.00am to 5.00pm, Monday to Saturday, with a 24-hour message answering service. Visit our website at www.hoddereducation.co.uk

First published in 2007 by
Hodder Education,
part of Hachette Livre UK,
338 Euston Road
London NW1 3BH

Impression number	10 9 8 7 6 5 4 3 2
Year	2012 2011 2010 2009 2008

Cover photo © Cosmopolitan Book Corporation/Images.com/Corbis
Typeset in Frutiger Light/Caslon Book BE Italic by Servis Filmsetting Ltd, Stockport, Cheshire
Printed in Spain

A catalogue record for this title is available from the British Library

ISBN: 978 0 340 94086 0

Contents

Daniel Defoe

Introduction

The book ***Robinson Crusoe*** was written in 1719 by Daniel Defoe. It was the first novel ever written! Before then, people liked to read true-life stories, news and views, and poetry.

Daniel Defoe

Daniel Defoe was the son of a London butcher. He was born around 1660, about 50 years after the death of Shakespeare, when Charles II was on the throne. Defoe lived in the Stuart period. We know that he travelled widely in Spain, Italy, France and Germany, that he was active in politics, and had strong views about religion. He disliked the hard-line attitudes of those in power and wrote poems and articles about the need for greater tolerance. On one occasion in 1703, his writing upset the authorities and he was imprisoned and pilloried. People saw him as a hero, but it seems that the experience made him bitter. He lost friends, confidence and money. The next part of his life was spent in shady jobs. He was a spy and a secret agent, a bankrupt, a prisoner and an amazing writer. Even his employers didn't trust him. He was often in trouble.

Daniel Defoe didn't start writing novels until he was in his late 50s. *Robinson Crusoe* was published in 1719 when he was 59. It was not his only success. He went on to write *Moll Flanders* and *A Journal of the Plague Year*, scores of pamphlets on current affairs and more novels and non-fiction books. One was a grand tour of the British Isles, and another was called *The Complete English Gentleman*. Altogether he wrote over 250 works, most of them in his old age.

Robinson Crusoe

Robinson Crusoe was based on the true story of Alexander Selkirk. Selkirk ran away from home and joined a ship's crew heading across the world to South America. At his own request, he was put ashore on an uninhabited island in the Juan Fernandez group of islands off the coast of Chile. He stayed there for 5 years until he was rescued by a passing ship. Defoe borrowed from Selkirk's own account of his life on the island but added to it from his imagination.

Alexander Selkirk

People at the time were used to reading real-life accounts, but Defoe did something new and unusual in making up a fictional account which sounded like real life. At first people assumed it was a true story, and didn't believe it could be fiction. Fiction was something they expected to see in plays or read in poems. Fiction was just fairy tales for children.

Robinson Crusoe is often described as the first novel ever written. It is longer and more rambling than a modern novel. For example, it contains stories from Crusoe's youth, and continues long after the shipwreck story is finished. In fact, the publisher rejected the novel when it first arrived. They simply didn't think it would sell.

The diary

The part of the novel you will read in this book is the diary of Robinson Crusoe during his early months on the island. His ship has been wrecked in a storm and, as the dead bodies are washed ashore, Robinson Crusoe realises he is the only survivor. From nothing, he has to find food, shelter and a way of coping with his loneliness. The diary is one of the ways he keeps himself occupied and stays sane.

Once his ink runs out, the diary ends, but the story continues if you want to find it in the full text. The language is old, and won't be easy at first, but it is surprising that you do get used to it if you persevere.

In the rest of the story, Robinson Crusoe builds a home and spends long years alone. The most famous moment of the novel is when Crusoe finds a footprint in the sand and realises that someone else has set foot on the island. With a new companion, Crusoe defends his island from villains, and is finally rescued by a passing ship after 28 years and 9 months.

THE FOOTPRINT IN THE SAND.

Robinson Crusoe finds a footprint in the sand.

Robinson Crusoe's Diary

September 30th, 1659

I, poor miserable Robinson Crusoe, being shipwrecked during a dreadful storm, came on shore on this dismal island, which I called 'The Island of Despair'; all the rest being drowned. I had neither food, house, clothes, weapon, nor place to fly to; and in despair, saw nothing but death before me. At night I slept in a tree, for fear of wild creatures; but slept soundly, though it rained all night.

All these days spent in many several voyages to get all I could out of the ship, upon rafts.

October 1st

In the morning I saw, to my great surprise, the ship had floated with the high tide, and was much nearer the island. I hoped I might get on board, and get some food and necessaries out. It renewed my grief at the loss of my comrades. I went upon the sand as near as I could, and then swam on board.

From the 1st of October to the 24th

All these days spent in many several voyages to get all I could out of the ship, upon rafts. Much rain also in the days; it seems this was the rainy season.

October 20th

I overset my raft, and all the goods I had upon it; I recovered many of them when the tide was out.

October 25th

It rained all night and all day, with some gusts of wind; the ship broke in pieces, and was no more to be seen, except the wreck at low water. I spent this day in covering the goods I had saved, that the rain might not spoil them.

October 26th

I walked about the shore almost all day, to find out a place to secure myself from any attack in the night, from wild beasts or men. I fixed upon a place under a rock and marked out a semicircle for my camp.

From the 26th to the 30th I worked very hard in carrying all my goods to my new habitation, though it rained hard.

The 31st, in the morning, I went out with my gun to seek for some food, and discover the country. I killed a she-goat, and her kid followed me home, which I afterwards killed also, because it would not feed.

November 1st

I set up my tent under a rock, and lay there for the first night; making it as large as I could, with stakes driven in to swing my hammock upon.

November 2nd

I set up all my chests and pieces of timber and formed a fence round me.

November 3rd

I went out with my gun, and killed two fowls like ducks, which were very good food. In the afternoon went to work to make me a table.

November 4th

This morning I began to order my times of work, of going out with my gun, and my time of sleep. Every morning I walked out with my gun for two or three hours, if it did not rain; then worked till about eleven o'clock; then ate what I had to live on; and from twelve to two I lay down to sleep, the weather being hot; and then, in the evening, to work again.

November 5th

This day went with my gun and my dog, and killed a wild cat; her skin pretty soft, but her flesh good for nothing; every creature that I killed I took off the skins and preserved them. Coming back by the sea-shore, I saw two or three seals, which got into the sea, and escaped me.

I went to work with my table again, and finished it.

November 6th

After my morning walk I went to work with my table again, and finished it, though not to my liking; nor was it long before I learned to mend it.

November 7th

Now it began to be settled fair weather. The 7th, 8th, 9th, 10th, and part of the 12th (for the 11th was Sunday) I took to make me a chair, and even in the making I pulled it in pieces several times.

November 13th

This day it rained, with terrible thunder and lightning.

November 14th, 15th and 16th

These three days I spent in making boxes, which might hold about a pound of powder. On one of these three days I killed a large bird that was good to eat, but I knew not what to call it.

November 17th

This day I began to dig behind my tent into the rock, to make room.

November 18th

The next day, in searching the woods, I found a tree which they call the iron-tree, for its exceeding hardness. Almost spoiling my axe, I cut a piece and brought it home with difficulty, for it was exceeding heavy. I worked it little and little into the form of a shovel or spade; the handle exactly shaped like ours in England, only that the board part, it would not last me so long; but never was a shovel made after that fashion, or so long in making. I wanted a basket or a wheelbarrow. A basket I could not make, having no such things as twigs that would bend; and as to a wheelbarrow, I fancied I could make all but the wheel; but I had no way to make the axis of the wheel; so I gave it over.

November 23rd

Working every day, as my strength and time allowed, I spent eighteen days in widening and deepening my cave, that it might hold my goods. Sometimes, in the wet season of the year, it rained so hard that I could not keep myself dry, which caused me to cover all my place with long poles, leaning against the rock, and load them with flags and large leaves of trees, like a thatch.

December 10th

I began now to think my cave finished, when on a sudden earth fell down from the top on one side; so much that it frighted me, and not without reason, for if I had been under it, I had never wanted a gravedigger. I had a great deal of work to do over again, for I had the loose earth to carry out and I had the ceiling to prop up, so no more would come down.

December 11th

I finished the next day, and in about a week, I had the roof secured, and the posts, standing in rows, served to part off the house.

I began now to think my cave finished.

December 17th

From this day to the 20th I placed shelves, and knocked up nails on the posts, to hang everything up that could be hung up; and now I began to be in some order within doors.

December 20th

Now I carried everything into the cave, and began to furnish my house, and I made me another table.

December 24th

Much rain all night and all day. No stirring out.

December 25th

Rain all day.

December 26th

No rain, and the earth much cooler than before, and pleasanter.

December 27th

Killed a young goat, and lamed another, so that I caught it and led it home in a string; when I had it at home, I bound and splintered up its leg, which was broke. I took such care of it that it lived, and the leg grew well and as strong as ever; but, by my nursing it so long, it grew tame, and fed upon the little green at my door, and would not go away. This was the first time that I thought of breeding up some tame creatures, that I might have food when my powder and shot was all spent.

December 28th, 29th, 30th and 31st

Great heats, and no breeze, so that there was no stirring, except in the evening, for food.

January 1st

Very hot still: but I went with my gun, and lay still in the middle of the day. This evening, going farther into the valleys which lay towards the centre of the island, I found there were plenty of goats, though shy, and hard to come at; however, I resolved to bring my dog to hunt them down.

January 2nd

The next day I went out with my dog, and set him upon the goats, but I was mistaken, for they all faced about upon the dog, and he knew his danger too well, for he would not come near them.

January 3rd

I began my fence or wall; which I resolved to make very thick and strong. I worked very hard, the rains hindering me many days, nay, sometimes weeks together; but I thought I should never be secure till this wall was finished.

During this time I made my rounds in the woods for game every day. I found a kind of wild pigeon, which build not in a tree but in the holes of the rocks; and taking some young ones, I endeavoured to breed them up tame, and did so; but when they grew older they flew away, for I had nothing to give them; however, I found their nests, and got their young ones, which were very good meat.

And now I found myself wanting in many things. I was at a great loss for candles; so that as soon as ever it was dark, which was by seven o'clock, I was obliged to go to bed. When I had killed a goat, I saved the tallow, and with a little dish made of clay, which I baked in the sun, I added a wick and this gave me light, though not a clear, steady light, like a candle.

During this time I made my rounds in the woods for game every day.

Rummaging my things, I found a little bag which had been filled with corn for feeding of poultry. I saw nothing in the bag but husks and dust. I shook the husks of corn out of it, under the rock. It was a little before the great rains I threw this stuff away, taking no notice, and not remembering that I had thrown anything there, when, about a month after, I saw some few stalks of something green shooting out of the ground, which I fancied might be some plant I had not seen; but I was astonished, when, after a little time, I saw ten or twelve ears come out, which were perfect green barley.

It is impossible to express my thoughts. But after I saw barley grow there, in a climate which I knew was not proper for corn, I began to suggest that God had caused grain to grow without seed. This touched my heart, and brought tears out of my eyes, and I began to bless myself that nature should happen upon my account.

I went all over that part of the island, where I had been before, peering in every corner, and under every rock, to see for more of it, but I could not find any.

I carefully saved the ears of this corn, you may be sure, in their season, which was about the end of June; and, laying up every corn, I resolved to sow them all again, hoping in time to have some bread. But it was not till the fourth year that I could allow myself the least grain of this corn to eat, for I lost all that I sowed the first season by not observing the proper time; for I sowed it just before the dry season, so that it never came up at all.

I worked hard these three or four months to get my wall done; and the 14th of April I closed it up.

April 16th

I finished the ladder; so I went up the ladder to the top, and then pulled it up after me, and let it down in the inside. This was a complete enclosure. Nothing could come at me unless it could first mount my wall.

The very next day after this wall was finished I had almost had all my labour overthrown at once, and myself killed. As I was busy in the inside, just at the entrance into my cave, I was terribly frighted with a most dreadful, surprising thing; for all on a sudden I found the earth come crumbling down from the roof of my cave, and two of the posts I had set up in the cave cracked in a frightful manner. I was heartily scared, thinking that the top of my cave was fallen in, and for fear I should be buried in it. I ran forward to my ladder, and got over my wall. It was a terrible earthquake, for the ground I stood on shook three times, with three such shocks as would have overturned the strongest; and a great piece of the top of a rock which stood about half a mile from me next the sea fell down with such a terrible noise as I never heard in all my life. The very sea was put into violent motion by it; and I believe the shocks were stronger under the water than on the island.

I was so amazed, having never felt the like, that I was like one dead or stupefied; and the motion of the earth made my stomach sick, like one that was tossed at sea; but the noise of the falling of the rock filled me with horror; and I thought of nothing then but the hill falling and burying all at once; and this sunk my very soul within me.

After the third shock was over, and I felt no more for some time, I began to take courage; and yet I had not heart enough to go over my wall again, for fear of being buried alive, but sat still upon the ground cast down, not knowing what to do.

I had not heart enough to go over my wall again . . . but sat still upon the ground cast down.

The wind blew a most dreadful hurricane; the sea was all on a sudden covered over with foam and froth.

While I sat thus, I found the air overcast and cloudy, as if it would rain. Soon after that the wind arose by little and little, so that in less than half-an-hour it blew a most dreadful hurricane; the sea was all on a sudden covered over with foam and froth; the shore was covered with the breach of the water, the trees were torn up by the roots, and a terrible storm it was. This held about three hours; and in two hours more it was quite calm, and began to rain very hard. I was forced to go into my cave, though very much afraid and uneasy. After I had been in my cave for some time, I went to my little store, and took a small sup of rum, knowing I could have no more when that was gone. It continued raining all that night and a great part of the next day but I began to think of what I had best do. I must consider building a little hut in an open place which I might surround with a wall, as I had done here, and make myself secure. I would go to work with all speed to build a wall in a circle, as before, and set my tent up in it but that I would stay where I was till it was finished, and fit to move.

April 22nd

The next morning I was at a great loss about my tools. I had three large axes and hatchets but they were all full of notches, and dull; and though I had a grindstone, I could not turn it and grind my tools. This cost me as much thought as a statesman would have upon a grand point of politics, or a judge upon the life and death of a man. I contrived a wheel with a string, to turn it with my foot, that I might have both my hands at liberty.

April 28th and 29th

These two whole days I took up in grinding my tools, my machine for turning my grindstone performing very well.

April 30th

Having perceived my bread had been low a great while, now I took a survey of it, and reduced myself to one biscuit cake a day, which made my heart very heavy.

May 1st

In the morning, looking towards the sea, I saw something on the shore bigger than ordinary, and it looked like a cask; when I came to it, I found a small barrel, and two or three pieces of the wreck of the ship, which were driven on shore by the hurricane; and looking towards the wreck itself, it seemed to lie higher out of the water than it used to do. I examined the barrel, and soon found it was a barrel of gunpowder; but it had taken water, and the powder was caked as hard as a stone; however, I rolled it on shore, and went as near as I could to the wreck of the ship, to look for more. I found it strangely moved. The forecastle was heaved up at least six feet, and the stern, which was broke in pieces by the force of the sea, was cast on one side; and the sand was thrown so high that I could now walk up to her when the tide was out. Many things came daily on shore, which the sea had loosened, and which the winds and water rolled to the land. The inside of the ship was choked up with sand.

May 3rd

I began with my saw, and cut a beam which held some of the deck together, and when I had cut it, I cleared away the sand as well as I could; but the tide coming in, I was obliged to give over for that time.

May 4th

I went a-fishing, but caught not one fish that I durst eat; when, just going to leave off, I caught a young dolphin. I had a long line of rope but I had no hooks; yet I caught as much as I cared to eat; all which I dried in the sun, and ate them dry.

May 5th

Worked on the wreck; cut another beam, and brought three great planks off from the decks, which I tied together, and made to float on shore when the tide came on.

May 6th

Worked on the wreck; got several iron bolts out of her and other pieces of ironwork. Worked very hard, and came home very much tired, and had thoughts of giving it over.

May 7th

Went to the wreck again, not with an intent to work, but found the wreck had broke itself down; pieces of the ship seemed to lie loose, and the inside of the hold lay so open that I could see into it; but it was almost full of water and sand.

Went every day to the wreck; and got a great many pieces of timber and iron.

May 8th

Went to the wreck, and wrenched open two planks, and brought them on shore with the tide.

May 9th

Went to the wreck, and made way into the body of the wreck, and felt several casks, and loosened them, but could not break them up. I felt also a roll of English lead, but it was too heavy to move.

May 10th to 14th

Went every day to the wreck; and got a great many pieces of timber and iron.

May 15th

I carried two hatchets, to try if I could cut a piece off the roll of lead by placing the edge of one hatchet and driving it with the other; but as it lay about a foot and a half in the water, I could not make any blow to drive the hatchet.

May 16th

It had blown hard in the night, and the wreck appeared more broken by the force of the water; but I stayed so long in the woods, to get pigeons for food, that the tide prevented my going to the wreck that day.

May 17th

I saw some pieces of the wreck blown on shore, at a great distance, near two miles off me, and found it was a piece of the head, but too heavy for me to bring away.

May 24th

Every day, to this day, I worked on the wreck; and I loosened some things so much, that at the first tide, several casks floated out, and two of the seamen's chests; but the wind blowing from the shore, nothing came to land that day but pieces of timber, and a hogshead, which had some pork in it; but the salt water and the sand had spoiled it.

June 16th

Going down to the seaside, I found a large tortoise or turtle. This was the first I had seen, for I happened to be on the other side of the island. I might have had hundreds of them every day, as I found afterwards.

June 17th

I spent in cooking the turtle. I found in her three-score eggs; and her flesh was to me, at that time, the most savoury and pleasant that ever I tasted in my life, having had no flesh, but of goats and fowls, since I landed in this horrid place.

June 18th

Rained all day, and I stayed within. I thought at this time the rain felt cold, and I was something chilly; which I knew was not usual.

June 19th

Very ill, and shivering, as if the weather had been cold.

June 20th

No rest all night; violent pains in my head, and feverish.

June 21st

Very ill; frighted almost to death - to be sick, and no help. Prayed to God, for the first time, but scarce knew what I said, or why.

No rest all night; violent pains in my head, and feverish.

June 22nd
A little better.

June 23rd
Very bad again; cold and shivering, and then a violent headache.

June 24th
Much better.

June 25th
A fit held me seven hours; cold fit and hot, with faint sweats after it.

June 26th
Better; took my gun, but found myself very weak. However, I killed a she-goat, and with much difficulty got it home, and broiled some of it, and ate. I would have stewed it, and made some broth, but had no pot.

June 27th

I lay a-bed all day, and neither ate nor drank. I was ready to perish for thirst; but so weak, I had not strength to stand up, or to get myself any water to drink. Prayed to God again, but was light-headed; and when I was not, I was so ignorant that I knew not what to say; only I lay and cried, 'Lord, look upon me! Lord, pity me! Lord, have mercy upon me!' I suppose I did nothing else for two or three hours till I fell asleep, and did not wake till far in the night. When I awoke, I found myself much refreshed, but weak, and thirsty. However, as I had no water, I was forced to lie till morning, and went to sleep again.

In this second sleep I had this terrible dream: I thought that I was sitting on the ground, on the outside of my wall, and that I saw a man descend from a great black cloud, in a bright flame of fire, and light upon the ground. He was all over as bright as a flame, so that I could but just bear to look towards him. When he stepped upon the ground with his feet, I thought the earth trembled, just as it had done before in the earthquake, and all the air looked as if it had been filled with flashes of fire. He was no sooner landed upon the earth, but he moved forward towards me, with a long spear or weapon in his hand, to kill me. I heard a voice 'Thou shalt die;' at which words, he lifted up the spear. Then I cried out, 'Lord, be my help, for I am in great distress.' This was the first prayer, if I may call it so, that I had made for many years.

June 28th

Having been refreshed with sleep, and the fit being off, I got up; and the first thing I did, I filled a large square case-bottle with water, and set it upon my table, in reach of my bed; and I put about a quarter of a pint of rum into it, and mixed them together. Then I got a piece of the goat's flesh and broiled it on the coals, but could eat very little. I walked about, but was very weak and very sad and heavy-hearted. At night I made my supper of three of the turtle's eggs, which I roasted in the ashes, and ate, in the shell, and this was the first bit of meat I had ever asked God's blessing to, that I could remember, in my whole life.

After I had eaten I tried to walk, but found myself so weak that I could hardly carry a gun, for I never went out without that; so I went but a little way, and sat down upon the ground, looking out upon the sea, which was just before me, and very calm and smooth.

As I sat here some such thoughts as these occurred to me: What is this earth and sea, of which I have seen so much? Whence is it produced? And what am I, and all the other creatures wild and tame, human and brutal? Whence are we? Sure we are all made by some secret Power, who formed the earth and sea, the air and sky. And who is that? Then it followed most naturally, it is God that has made all. He knows that I am here, and am in this dreadful condition. Why has God done this to me? What have I done to be thus used? My conscience spoke to me like a voice: 'Wretch! dost THOU ask what thou hast done? Look back upon a misspent life, and ask what thou hast NOT done? Ask, why is it that thou wert not long ago destroyed? Why wert thou not drowned, when all the crew perished but thyself? Dost THOU ask, what have I done?'

I had not a word to say – no, but rose up sad, walked back and went up over my wall, as if I had been going to bed; but I had no sleep; so I sat down in my chair, and lighted my lamp, for it began to be dark. It grew now late, and I dozed. But before I lay down, I did what I never had done in all my life – I kneeled down, and prayed to God to fulfil the promise to me, that if I called upon Him in the day of trouble, He would deliver me.

I fell into a sound sleep, and waked no more till the afternoon the next day – nay, to this hour I am partly of opinion that I slept all the next day and night, and till almost three the day after; for otherwise I know not how I should lose a day out of my reckoning in the days of the week, as it appeared some years after I had done. When I awaked I found myself refreshed, and my spirits lively and cheerful; when I got up I was stronger than I was the day before, and my stomach better, for I was hungry. I had altered for the better.

Glossary

overset	overturned
pilloried	punished by being locked to a post in public
powder	gunpowder
reckoning	adding up
shot	lead pellets like bullets
splintered up	set in a splint
stern	back end of the ship
three-score	$3 \times 20 = 60$
wanted	lacked, needed
whence?	from where?

Jesus With Us

Coloring Stories About Jesus For Children

for

EASTER * PENTECOST and THE EARLY CHURCH

written and illustrated by
Judi Hibel Winkowski

St Paul Publications

Text design by Ellen Whitney

ISBN: 085439 291 2

First published in the United States of America by Paulist Press, 997 Macarthur Boulevard, Mahwah, New Jersey 07430, and published in England by St. Paul Publications, Middlegreen, Slough SL3 6BT and in Australia by St. Paul Publications, 60-70 Broughton Road, Homebush NSW 2140. St. Paul Publications is an activity of the priests and brothers of the Society of St. Paul who proclaim the Gospel through the media of social communication.

Printed and Bound in the United States of America

JESUS WITH US is one of a series of four coloring stories about the life of Jesus. It has been lovingly prepared for school age children.

The stories are adapted from the New Testament, with scriptural references, and follow the liturgical calendar for the seasons of

EASTER ★ PENTECOST
and includes THE EARLY CHURCH

Other coloring stories in the series are:

JESUS COMES	Advent ★ Christmas Epiphany
NEW LIFE IN JESUS	Lent
JESUS SHOWS US HIS LOVE	Ordinary Time

The Risen Lord!

On the first day of the week, at sunrise, three women came with anointing oils to the tomb where Jesus had been buried. They were puzzled to see the large, heavy stone to the entrance rolled away. They cautiously peered inside and saw a young man in a white robe sitting there. He told them to be glad, for Jesus had risen from the dead. The women excitedly went to tell the disciples, Jesus' friends, the wonderful news. Jesus had risen just as he had promised!

read Matthew 28:1–8

Breakfast By The Sea

After Jesus came back to life on Easter morning, he went to the Sea of Tiberias to see his friends. They were out in their boats, fishing. He called to them to bring in their catch and have breakfast with him. They cooked bread and fish over an open fire, and shared it, happy to be with one another again.

read John 21:9–13

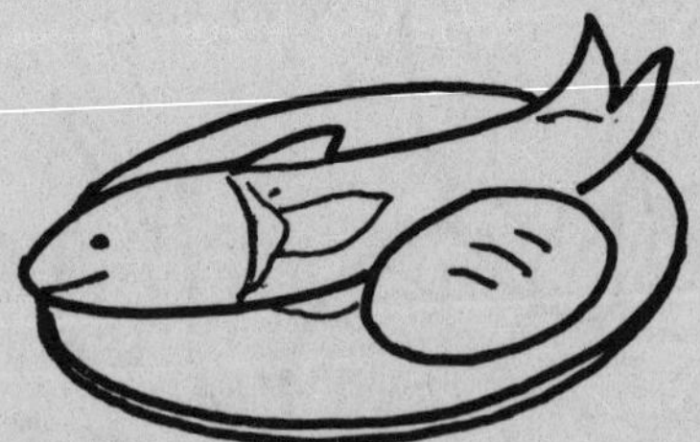

Jesus Goes Back To The Father

After rising from the dead, Jesus was with his friends and helpers. He took them to a place called Bethany. There he spoke to them about the kingdom of God. He reminded them how John the Baptist had baptized them with water. Jesus promised his friends that soon they would be baptized with the Holy Spirit. As he was blessing them he was lifted up. Jesus went back to heaven to prepare a place for us.

read Luke 24:50–53
John 14:1–3

The Spirit Comes

Jesus' close friends, the disciples, came together to pray. Suddenly they heard a sound like a rushing wind. They saw what looked like tongues of fire over each other's heads. The disciples were not frightened, because they remembered what Jesus had promised them about the coming of the Holy Spirit. Great peace and happiness filled their hearts. The Spirit was within them to keep them strong. Now the disciples became known as the apostles because they were "sent out" to tell everyone about Jesus.

read Acts 2:1–3

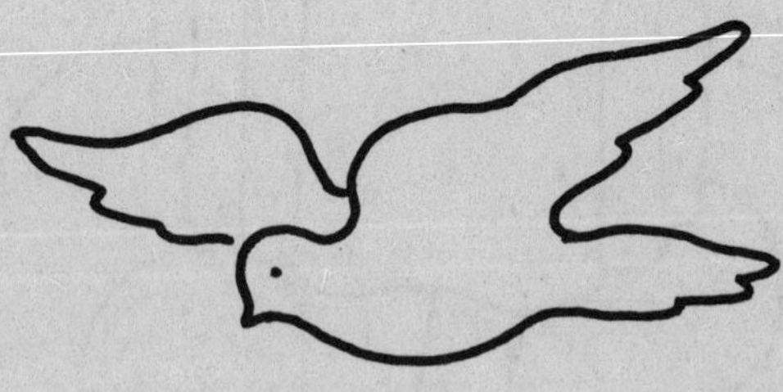

The First Christian Church

Through the Holy Spirit, the apostles were given the power to heal, and to perform many miracles. The apostles baptized many people. The new followers were called Christians. Peter, one of the apostles, became the leading member of the community. The new Christians shared all they had with one another. They broke bread and prayed together, praising God for their new life.

read Acts 2:42–47

The Story Of Paul

Among those who were baptized in the Christian faith was Saul, a Roman citizen. At first, Saul was against the idea of the early Church. He arrested many Christians, and had them punished. As Saul traveled one day to Damascus, a bright light flashed around him. He fell to the ground, blinded. God loved Saul, and wanted him to help spread his word to far-away places. Saul heard God speak to him. Something inside Saul changed. He was able to see again. He took the name Paul, and joined the apostles in their work of telling others about Jesus.

read Acts 9:1–19

The Apostles Share The Good News

As Jesus had instructed them, the apostles went out to preach the good news to all people. They shared with others all that Jesus had taught them about love, forgiveness and new life. The message the apostles brought was for everyone. People found great joy and hope in what they heard. Many were baptized, and soon there were Christian communities in Palestine, in Asia, in Greece, and in Rome.

read Mark 16:15
Acts 11:19–26

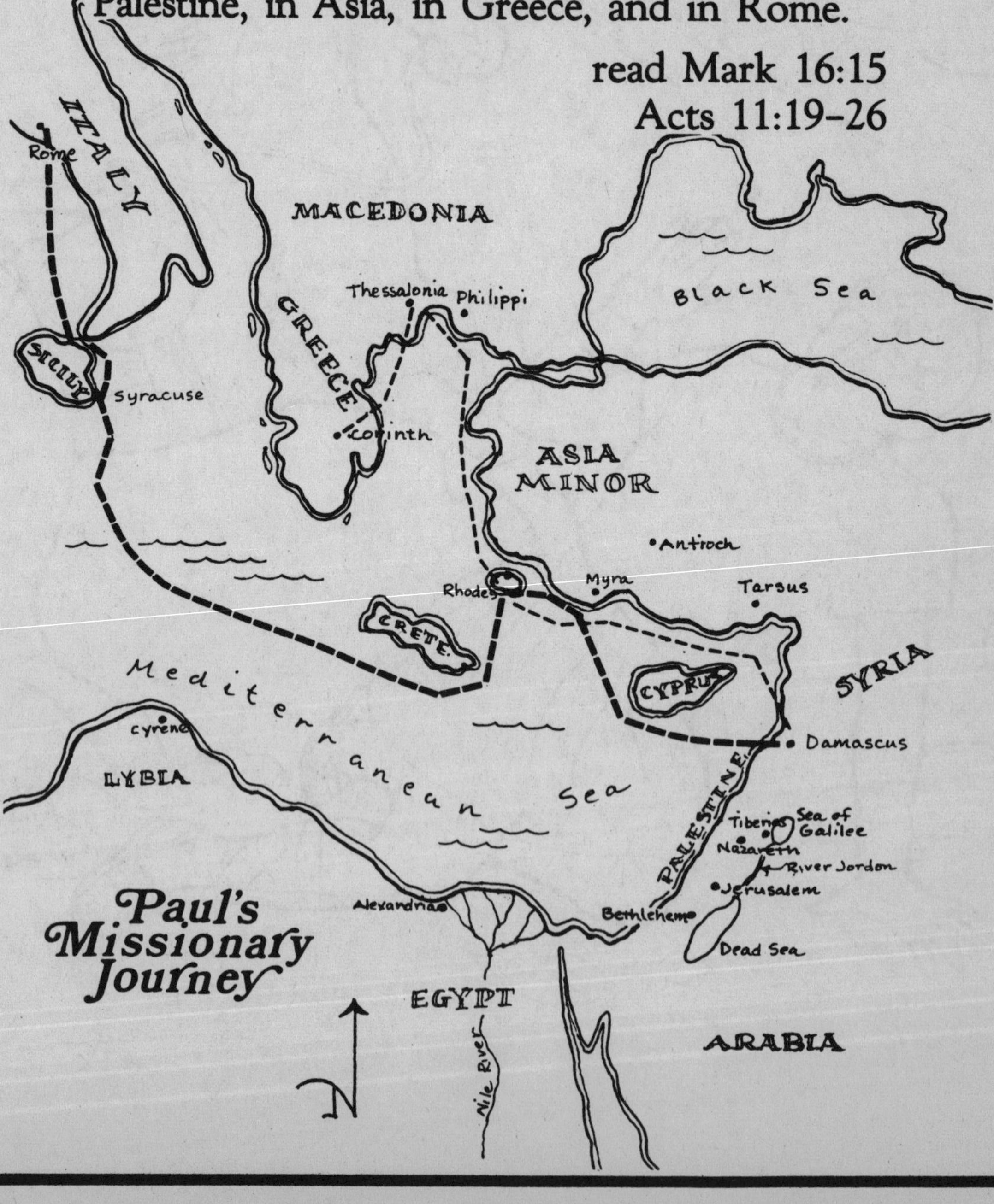